D1047851

Scripture Confessions
for HEALING

LIFE-CHANGING WORDS OF FAITH
FOR EVERY DAY

HARRISON HOUSE
Tulsa, Oklahoma

12 11 10 09   14 13 12 11 10

Scripture Confessions for Healing:
Life-Changing Words of Faith for Every Day
ISBN 13: 978-1-57794-873-5
ISBN 10: 1-57794-873-4
Copyright © 2007 by Word & Spirit Resources
P.O. Box 701403
Tulsa, Oklahoma 74170

Published by Harrison House, Inc.
P.O. Box 35035
Tulsa, Oklahoma 74153

CONTENTS

INTRODUCTION

God's Word makes it perfectly clear that it is God's will that you are to be well, healthy, and whole. The same blood that Jesus shed on Calvary's tree for your redemption was also shed that you might be free from sickness and disease. Matthew 8:17 says that Jesus Himself bore our sicknesses and carried our diseases. He did that for you; and if He carried them for you, then you don't have to carry them. Healing is God's promise to you. But just because it's God's will for your life doesn't mean it will automatically happen. You have to believe His promises, reach out for them in faith, and snatch them for yourself. Everything you receive from God you receive by faith. A key factor in releasing your faith is the words that come out of your mouth. There is power released into your life when you speak God's Word. It is a vital part of appropriating God's promises and activating spiritual forces that will bring God's promises to manifestation.

Jesus said in Mark 11:23-24 that "whosoever shall *say* unto this mountain, Be thou removed, and be thou cast into the sea; and shall not doubt in his heart, but shall believe that those things which he *saith* shall come to pass; he shall have whatsoever he *saith*. Therefore I say unto you, What things soever ye desire, when ye pray, believe that ye receive them, and ye shall have them." Speak to the mountain in your life and it will obey you! Wow! Isn't that awesome?

The confessions in this book are faith declarations based on God's Word. I encourage you to speak them daily over your life. No matter what kind of sickness or health challenge you are going through, there is hope, there is help, there is strength, and there is life-altering power in speaking God's Word. Be faithful to speak His Word. Release your faith as you speak, and say these declarations boldly. Speak with power and authority. Even if you are hurting, even if you are afraid, even if you are too weak to lift your head, speak the Word with confidence. Release your faith and lay claim to the healing that is rightfully yours.

Now, start speaking—and get ready to experience God's healing power in your life!

Start the Day With God

This is the day that the Lord has made, and I will rejoice and be glad in it. I start every day with God by speaking life, health, strength, and vitality into my body because I know God's healing power is at work within me. The nature and life of God are resident in my body, driving out all manner of sickness and disease. I am strong in the Lord and in the power of His might. I believe the Word of God above anything that I think, feel, or see. His Word says that I have been redeemed from the curse of sickness. His Word says that by Jesus' stripes I am healed.

My body is free from pain, sickness, and disease. It operates effectively and efficiently— free from malfunction of any kind. Every part of my body is functioning properly. Every organ, gland, and system is operating in conjunction with each other in perfect harmony, which is exactly how God designed my body to work. My immune system is strong, vibrant, and healthy. Germs, bacteria, viruses, and parasites cannot exist in my body. If any sickness or disease makes any attempt to try and attack my body, then it is quickly destroyed by the power of God's Word working in me. I boldly declare that I am healed, healthy, and whole.

Scriptures

This is the day which the Lord hath made; we will rejoice and be glad in it.

Psalm 118:24

He was wounded for our transgressions, he was bruised for our iniquities; the chastisement of our peace was upon him; and with his stripes we are healed.

Isaiah 53:5

Be strong in the Lord, and in the power of his might.

Ephesians 6:10

Christ hath redeemed us from the curse of the law, being made a curse for us: for it is written, Cursed is every one that hangeth on a tree.

Galatians 3:13

Supernatural Strength

I am strong in the Lord and in the power of His might. The joy of the Lord is my strength, and His strength sustains me. I am full of energy; I am vibrant and full of life and vitality. God in me is stronger than any weakness in my flesh. It doesn't matter how I feel because I am not moved by feelings. I speak supernatural strength, energy, and vitality to my body. Weakness, tiredness, and weariness, I command you to get out of my body.

I can do all things through Christ who strengthens me. I have dynamic energy and indomitable strength. I am undaunted in my faith; I am strong in the Lord. I am courageous and fearless.

Greater is He that is in me than He that is in the world. His strength rises up in me; He puts me above my feelings. I am strong in my spirit, I am strong in my mind, and I am strong in my body.

My strength is renewed like the eagle's. God increases my strength; therefore, I am not weary.

Scriptures

The joy of the Lord is your strength.
                                                    Nehemiah 8:10

I can do all things through Christ which strengtheneth me.
                                                    Philippians 4:13

Greater is he that is in you, than he that is in the world.
                                                    1 John 4:4

Bless the Lord...who satisfieth thy mouth with good things; so that thy youth is renewed like the eagle's.
                                                    Psalm 103:1,5

He gives power to the weak, And to those who have no might He increases strength.
                                                    Isaiah 40:29

Be strong and courageous! ...Do not be afraid or discouraged, for the Lord will personally go ahead of you. He will be with you; he will neither fail you nor abandon you.
                                                    Deuteronomy 31:7,8 NLT

I Will Not Give Up

Even though I may be surrounded by oppressors, I am never smothered or crushed by them. I may suffer embarrassments and become perplexed, and it may seem that there is no way out, but I still will not be driven to despair. Even though I may be pursued, persecuted, and hard driven, God will never desert me and make me stand alone. Even though I may be struck down to the ground, I will never be struck out or destroyed. No matter what difficulties or obstacles may come my way, I will never, never, never quit!

I will not faint in the time of adversity because God is with me. I am strong and very courageous. I am persistent and undaunted in my faith. I shall never quit and I will not yield. I will not bow my knee to sickness. I am steadfast and unmovable. I am valiant and fearless, determined and resolute in my faith. I am strong in the Lord and in the power of His might. No weapon formed against me shall prosper. I will not lose heart; I will not weaken or cave in. Victory is mine. I am relentless in my pursuit of total and complete wellness and wholeness for my body.

Scriptures

Thou shalt make thy way prosperous, and then thou shalt have good success. Have not I commanded thee? Be strong and of a good courage.

Joshua 1:8,9

[The Lord said] I will never leave thee, nor forsake thee.

Hebrews 13:5

For only we who believe can enter his rest.

Hebrews 4:3 NLT

We are hedged in (pressed) on every side [troubled and oppressed in every way], but not cramped or crushed; we suffer embarrassments and are perplexed and unable to find a way out, but not driven to despair; We are pursued (persecuted and hard driven), but not deserted [to stand alone]; we are struck down to the ground, but never struck out and destroyed; Always carrying about in the body the liability and exposure to the same putting to death that the Lord Jesus suffered, so that the [resurrection] life of Jesus also may be shown forth by and in our bodies.

2 Corinthians 4:8-10 AMP

Jesus Already Did It!

Matthew 8:17 declares that Jesus Himself bore my sicknesses and diseases. And since He already bore them, I don't have to. He was made sick so that I might be made well. He was beaten and bruised for me. He was my substitute, and He became sick so I wouldn't have to.

Isaiah 53:5 says by His stripes I was healed. That is past tense. If I was healed, then that means that healing is already mine today. All I have to do is receive it. Jesus already did it for me. It's already done. I don't have to get my healing; it was a gift from my Lord and Savior. Jesus did it for me. He was bruised for my iniquities, the chastisement of my peace was on Him, and by His stripes I am healed.

My healing was bought and paid for two thousand years ago. I am not sick and trying to get healed. I am already healed, and sickness is trying to take hold in my body. But I won't let it! I boldly proclaim that Jesus already did it! Therefore I am healed! Sickness has no right to stay in my body. I am healed, healthy, and whole in the mighty name of Jesus.

Scriptures

Surely he hath borne our griefs, and carried our sorrows; yet we did esteem him stricken, smitten of God, and afflicted. But he was wounded for our transgressions, he was bruised for our iniquities; the chastisement of our peace was upon him; and with his stripes we are healed.

Isaiah 53:4,5

Bless the Lord, O my soul, and forget not all his benefits: Who forgiveth all thine iniquities; who healeth all thy diseases; who redeemeth thy life from destruction; who crowneth thee with lovingkindness and tender mercies.

Psalm 103:2-4

For he hath made him to be sin for us, who knew no sin; that we might be made the righteousness of God in him.

2 Corinthians 5:21

Redeemed From the Curse

Galatians 3:13 says I have been redeemed from the curse of the law. That means that the law of life in Christ Jesus has set me free from the law of sin and death. Sickness is a curse. And by the power of the redemptive blood of Jesus Christ, the Anointed One, I have been set free from the curse of sickness. Sickness, you have no right to stay in my body. The chains and bonds of sickness and disease have been broken over my life. Through Christ Jesus, they have no power to hurt or harm me. I am free from their bondage and captivity because Jesus was made sick so that I might be made well. I am a child of the most high God, and healing is the bread of God's children.

The curse has been broken through the redemptive work of Jesus. Abraham's blessings are also mine, and they include health and healing for my body. So as I have been redeemed from the curse, it no longer has any power over me. Jesus has given me power, dominion, and authority over sickness and disease. I choose to exercise that authority and boldly proclaim that I am free of sickness and disease, and I walk in health, healing, and wholeness. I am strong, healthy, and full of strength and vitality—and I have been redeemed from the curse.

Scriptures

Christ had redeemed us from the curse of the law, being made a curse for us; for it is written, Cursed is every one that hangeth on a tree.

Galatians 3:13

The law of the Spirit of life in Christ Jesus hath made me free from the law of sin and death.

Romans 8:2

In whom we have redemption through his blood, the forgiveness of sins, according to the riches of his grace.

Ephesians 1:7

Organs, Systems, and Glands

I speak to every organ in my body and command all of them to operate and function at 100 percent efficiency, the way God made them. My heart is strong and healthy, every valve working in perfect harmony. My heart beats in perfect rhythm, all the blood vessels surrounding my heart are free from blockages of any kind. My liver, kidneys, and lungs all operate and function effectively and efficiently with no hindrances. All my organs function and perform their duties effectively. All my organs are healthy and whole—free from sickness, disease, growths, and tumors.

Every system in my body operates like a well-oiled machine. My nervous system, my electrical system, my circulatory system, my lymphatic system, my digestive system, and every other system operate in total and complete harmony with each other. They are free from sickness, disease, growths, or tumors of any kind.

I speak life and health to all the glands in my body. I proclaim that they are healthy and whole. My adrenal gland, thyroid gland, pituitary gland, and all other glands in my body operate and function at 100 percent efficiency—free from sickness, disease, growths, and tumors. My body is healed, healthy, and whole; I am full of vim, vigor, and vitality.

Scriptures

He sent his word, and healed them, and delivered them from their destructions.

Psalm 107:20

And ye shall serve the LORD your God, and he shall bless thy bread, and thy water; and I will take sickness away from the midst of thee.

Exodus 23:25

But if the Spirit of him that raised up Jesus from the dead dwell in you, he that raised up Christ from the dead shall also quicken your mortal bodies by his Spirit that dwelleth in you.

Romans 8:11

When You Receive a Bad Report

I am not shaken because of bad reports; I choose to believe the Lord's good report. Bad news doesn't faze me a bit because I have learned to trust God and believe His Word even in the midst of challenging circumstances. I don't deny that sickness exists; I just deny it has a right to exist in my body.

The word of men doesn't change the Word of God. I don't deny what the doctor's word says; I just deny that it is the final word, because God's Word supersedes the word of men. I choose to believe God's report that says Jesus paid for my healing as my substitute on the Cross. His report says the law of life in Christ Jesus has made me free from the law of sin and death. His report says that healing and health are my right and privilege. God's Word says that by Jesus' stripes I was healed, and that is the report I choose to believe. It doesn't matter what the doctor says; I am healed. It doesn't matter what the medical tests say; I am healed. It doesn't matter what my body says; I say I am healed. God's Word says that I am healed, and I believe it. That settles the matter.

Scriptures

So shall my word be that goeth forth out of my mouth: it shall not return unto me void, but it shall accomplish that which I please, and it shall prosper in the thing whereto I sent it.

Isaiah 55:11

That is might be fulfilled which was spoken by Esaias the prophet, saying, Himself took our infirmities, and bare our sicknesses.

Matthew 8:17 KJV

Finally, brethren, whatever things are true, whatever things are noble, whatever things are just, whatever things are pure, whatever things are lovely, whatever things are of good report, if there is any virtue and if there is anything praiseworthy—meditate on these things.

Philippians 4:8 NKJV

Overcoming Fear

I am strong and very courageous; I will not fear. I will not let fear impact my life. I am not afraid, because God's Word gives me boldness and audacity. I do not fear the devil, I fear no sickness, I fear no disease, I am not intimidated by sickness and disease, but they are intimidated by my faith in God's Word. My faith and trust in God and His Word destroys the power of fear. God has not given me a spirit of fear but of power and love and a sound mind.

I refuse to get stressed out; I refuse to worry or be anxious. I stand firm and fearless in my faith. I will not fear because God is *for* me, God is *with* me, and God is *in* me. When God is for me, then nothing can be against me. Because God is in me, I can conquer anything. I am bold in my faith and I refuse to let one ounce of fear enter my life. I shall not be afraid, for the Lord is my God. I shall not fear, because my confidence is in the Lord. No fear here, in Jesus' name!

Scriptures

Be strong and of a good courage.

Joshua 1:6

David said to Solomon his son, Be strong and of good courage, and do it: fear not, nor be dismayed: for the Lord God...will not fail thee.

1 Chronicles 28:20

Fear thou not; for I am with thee.

Isaiah 41:10

God hath not given us the spirit of fear; but of power, and of love, and of a sound mind.

2 Timothy 1:7

Peace I leave with you, my peace I give unto you: not as the world giveth, give I unto you. Let not your heart be troubled, neither let it be afraid.

John 14:27

As soon as Jesus heard the word that was spoken, he saith unto the ruler of the synagogue, Be not afraid, only believe.

Mark 5:36

Authority Over Satan

Jesus came that I may have abundant life, but Satan comes to steal, kill, and destroy. God's will for my life is health and wholeness. Satan's will for my life is destruction, disease, and death. I choose abundant life. I remind you, Satan, that Jesus has already defeated you and taken away your authority to harm me. And it's in His name that I boldly proclaim: Satan, you are under my feet. I resist you, and I stand steadfast in my faith. I expect you to turn tail and run the other way. In the name of Jesus, I command you to stop and desist in any and all attempts to put sickness or disease on my body.

I take authority over Satan and break the power of any curses or spells that have been spoken over my life. Witchcraft, black magic, and all the forces of darkness have no power to affect my body. I cast down and break the power of any strategies, maneuvers, or evil plots that the enemy has set in motion to bring destruction to my life. They shall all come to naught because no weapon formed against me will prosper!

Scriptures

The thief cometh not, but for to steal, and to kill, and to destroy: I am come that they might have life, and that they might have it more abundantly.

John 10:10

No weapon that is formed against thee shall prosper.

Isaiah 54:17

...I have set before you life and death, blessing and cursing: therefore choose life, that both thou and thy seed may live.

Deuteronomy 30:19

...He gave them power and authority to drive out all demons and to cure diseases.

Luke 9:1 NIV

Submit yourselves therefore to God. Resist the devil, and he will flee from you.

James 4:7

But thanks be to God, which giveth us the victory through our Lord Jesus Christ. Therefore, my beloved brethren, be ye stedfast, unmoveable, always abounding in the work of the Lord, forasmuch as ye know that your labour is not in vain in the Lord.

1 Corinthians 15:57,58

Speak to the Mountain

My words have power. Jesus said if I would speak to a mountain in my life and tell it to be plucked up and thrown into the sea it would have to obey me. So because Jesus said to do it, and because I am obedient to His commands, I speak to the mountain of sickness in my life.

Sickness, listen up, pay attention. I am talking to you! In the name of Jesus Christ, the Anointed One, I command you to be plucked up and thrown out of my life and body. You have no choice. You can't stay. You have to leave. There is no alternative, no other options. Pack your bags, hit the road, and don't come back anymore. Today's mountain is tomorrow's testimony. It doesn't matter how big the mountain is, and it doesn't matter how long the mountain has been there. What does matter is what Jesus says about the mountain. He said if I speak to the mountain, it has to obey me. My life is mountain free—no mountains of sickness and disease here. The mountain of sickness has been eradicated and eliminated from my life. I am healed, healthy, and whole in Jesus' name.

Scriptures

Whosoever shall say unto this mountain, Be thou removed, and be thou cast into the sea; and shall not doubt in his heart, but shall believe that those things which he saith shall come to pass; he shall have whatsoever he saith.

Mark 11: 23,24

So Jesus said to them, "Because of your unbelief; for assuredly, I say to you, if you have faith as a mustard seed, you will say to this mountain, 'Move from here to there,' and it will move; and nothing will be impossible for you.

Matthew 17:20 NKJV

And I will give unto thee the keys of the kingdom of heaven: and whatsoever thou shalt bind on earth shall be bound in heaven: and whatsoever thou shalt loose on earth shall be loosed in heaven.

Matthew 16:19

End the Day With God

The Spirit of the Lord is on me. He quickens me and gives me strength. In Him I find rest, comfort, and peace. Even in the midst of the storms of life, I am calm, cool, and collected because my mind is focused on Jesus. He keeps me in perfect peace. I have confidence in God's Word, and I trust Him to bring it to pass. I am assured that He will never leave me or forsake me.

I cast all my cares on Him; in obedience to God's Word, I choose not to worry or be anxious about anything. I will not allow myself to be fearful and troubled about any circumstance in my life. Health and healing are mine. Jesus paid the price for them and His Word says they're mine. I have released my faith, I have received my healing according to the promise of His Word, and now all that is left for me to do is rest in Him until the complete manifestation of healing comes to pass. My God has promised to give His beloved sweet sleep. Therefore, I receive a full night's sleep every night, and I fully expect to wake up in the morning refreshed, revitalized, and raring to go.

Scriptures

Thou wilt keep him in perfect peace, whose mind is stayed on thee; because he trusteth in thee.

Isaiah 26:3

(The Lord thy God is a merciful God;) he will not forsake thee.

Deuteronomy 4:31

When thou liest down, thou shalt not be afraid: yea, thou shalt lie down, and thy sleep shall be sweet.

Proverbs 3:24

[The Lord said] I will never leave thee, nor forsake thee.

Hebrews 13:5

PRAYER OF SALVATION

God loves you—no matter who you are, no matter what your past. God loves you so much that He gave His one and only begotten Son for you. The Bible tells us that "...whoever believes in him shall not perish but have eternal life" (John 3:16 NIV). Jesus laid down His life and rose again so that we could spend eternity with Him in heaven and experience His absolute best on earth. If you would like to receive Jesus into your life, say the following prayer out loud and mean it from your heart:

Heavenly Father, I come to You admitting that I am a sinner. Right now, I choose to turn away from sin, and I ask You to cleanse me of all unrighteousness. I believe that Your Son, Jesus, died on the cross to take away my sins. I also believe that He rose again from the dead so that I might be forgiven of my sins and made righteous through faith in Him. I call upon the name of Jesus Christ to be the Savior and Lord of my life. Jesus, I choose to follow You and ask that You fill me with the power of the Holy Spirit. I declare that right now I am a child of God. I am free from sin and full of the righteousness of God. I am saved in Jesus' name. Amen.

If you prayed this prayer to receive Jesus Christ as your Savior for the first time, please contact us on the Web at **www.harrisonhouse.com** to receive a free book.

Or you may write to us at
Harrison House
P.O. Box 35035 • Tulsa, Oklahoma 74153

Other Books Available
in the Scripture Confessions Series

Scripture Confessions
For Finances

Scripture Confessions
For Victorious Living

Scripture Confessions
For Moms

Scripture Confessions
For Dads

Scripture Confessions
For Kids

Scripture Confessions
Gift Collection (Leather)

Available at bookstores everywhere or visit
www.harrisonhouse.com.

A Beautiful Gift Edition to Set Life's Course for Victory!

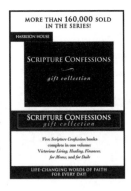

ISBN-13:
978-1-57794-916-9

God has given powerful promises in His Word—peace, joy, health, provision, and more. Let these promises become reality for you, a friend, or a loved one by agreeing with God's Word!

The *Scripture Confessions Gift Collection* includes five books complete in one volume: *Victorious Living, Healing, Finances,* and *for Parents.* This life-changing gift in beautiful Italian leather is a convenient and powerful Scripture resource designed to bring God's Word into busy lifestyles.

Available at fine bookstores everywhere or visit
www.harrisonhouse.com.

About the Authors

Keith and Megan Provance have been in Christian publishing for over 30 years, with Keith serving as President of Harrison House Publishing for 20 of those years. Together they founded Word and Spirit Resources, a company dedicated to the publishing and world-wide distribution of life changing books. Keith also works as a publishing consultant to national and international ministries.

Their book, *Pray for Our Nation*, has sold over 1.2 million copies and they have authored several other bestselling books including *Scripture Confessions for Victorious Living*, *Scripture Confessions for Healing*, and *Scripture Confessions for Finances*. They are the parents of three sons, Ryan, Garrett, and Jacob, and they reside in Tulsa, Oklahoma.

Fast. Easy.
Convenient.

For the latest Harrison House product informa-
tion and author news, look no further than
your computer. All the details on our powerful,
life-changing products are just a click away.
New releases, E-mail subscriptions, Podcasts,
testimonies, monthly specials—find it all in one
place. Visit harrisonhouse.com today!

harrisonhouse